A Ladybird Book

Jesus
the Leader

Text by Jenny Robertson
Illustrations by Alan Parry

Scripture Union/Ladybird

Out of the desert came a man called John. He
was sunburnt and strong. His hair was tangled
by the wind and he wore rough clothing made
from camel hair. He ate the food of the desert:
locusts, like grasshoppers, and wild honey. His
eyes glowed like the hot sun, and his voice,

strong as the wind, brought crowds to the banks of the River Jordan to hear him. 'You all do wrong things which make God angry!' John cried. 'Be sorry, and start to lead good lives. I shall baptise you here in the river as a sign that you are sorry. There isn't much time! We know that God has promised to give us a king to lead us. He will come soon, and we must be ready for him.'

One day Jesus came to the river and asked to be baptised, too. John knew that Jesus was God's promised king. Humbly he baptised Jesus. As they came up from the water they heard the voice of God himself: 'This is my own dear Son. I am very pleased with him.'

Then Jesus left the crowds on the river bank and went by himself into the desert where nothing grew. There was nowhere to shelter from the scorching sun or the bitter wind that blew at night. Wild animals roamed the desert and evil lurked there. When Jesus had been alone for forty days the Devil came to tempt Jesus. He wanted Jesus to use his power to win praise for himself instead of God.

He knew that Jesus had no food to eat. First of all he tried to make him turn the desert stones into bread. Jesus refused. 'Men need more than bread to stay alive,' he told the Devil. 'They need to know God's words and obey them, too.'

So the Devil took Jesus to the top of the Temple in Jerusalem and tested him again. 'Jump down! You won't hurt yourself. The holy writings teach that God will send angels to catch you.'

'The holy writings also teach that we must not test God,' Jesus replied. Then the Devil showed Jesus all the kingdoms of the world, with all their greatness and wealth. 'I will give all this to you if you will kneel down and worship me,' the Devil said. 'Go away, Devil,' said Jesus sternly. 'God is the only one to be worshipped!' Defeated, the Devil left, and God sent angels to Jesus to strengthen him after his temptation.

Two fishermen called Simon and Andrew were working with their nets, watched by some children. 'Jesus is coming this way!' the children said. 'We saw him back there, along the beach.'

Simon and Andrew looked up quickly. They had met Jesus before, and they wanted to talk to him again. Suddenly they heard his voice calling them: 'Simon! Andrew! Come with me! Leave your nets! I want you to help me tell everyone about God.'

At once the fishermen leapt to their feet. 'Goodbye, children!' they called, and set off happily after Jesus.

Nearby two more fishermen, James and John, were working in their boat with their father. James and John were Jesus' cousins.

'Come with us!' Jesus called them. 'I need your help, too.'

So the two men said goodbye to their father and went with Jesus.

Simon and Andrew lived in Capernaum, a town on the shore of the Sea of Galilee. 'Come home with us,' Simon invited Jesus. 'My wife and her mother will be so pleased to see you.' Simon did not know that his wife's mother was ill. They found her in bed. 'Oh, dear Teacher! I wanted to give you a proper welcome!' she cried when she saw Jesus. 'Then I felt so hot and weak I had to lie down.'

At once Jesus touched the old lady's hand to heal her. She felt better immediately. Without wasting any time she got up and cooked them all a delicious meal.

That evening, when the day's work was over, crowds of sick people gathered outside Simon's house. Mothers brought their babies. Children led their elderly, ailing grandparents. Those who couldn't walk were carried or helped along by friends. Blind people were guided. Sad people whose worries and problems made them sick came to Jesus. People who were

possessed by evil spirits came. Jesus helped them all. He touched the sick and made them well. He drove away the evil spirits. The people discovered that God cared about them and had sent Jesus to help them.

Now Jesus chose someone else to help him – Matthew, the tax-collector. Tax-collectors took money from the people to give the Romans who ruled the country. Often they cheated the

people, taking money for themselves, too. No one liked them, but Jesus went straight to the table where Matthew was working.

'Follow me!' he said. Matthew got up at once. He left his money bags and rolls of paper and hurried away with Jesus. That evening he held a party so that the other tax-collectors could meet Jesus. Some people were shocked to see Jesus mixing with such dishonest men, but Jesus explained, 'The bad people need me. In fact they are the ones I have come to help.'

The religious leaders were shocked and annoyed. They would never behave like Jesus did! Yet he claimed that he was doing what God wanted!

However, one of the leaders, a man called Nicodemus, was puzzled. He loved God, and wanted to know more about him. Many of the things that Jesus did and said seemed to prove that God was with him – he healed people, and

taught them wisely. So one night, after dark, when no one would see, he went to find Jesus. They talked together for a long time. Jesus answered Nicodemus' questions, and explained many things to him. At last Nicodemus went home, very thoughtfully. For a long time he told nobody, but secretly he had decided to become a follower of Jesus, too.

One day Jesus and his friends were travelling through a district called Samaria. It was hot, and while the others went to buy food, Jesus rested beside a well. A Samaritan woman came by for some water. She said nothing to Jesus, for Samaritans and Jews were enemies, and did not speak to one another. To her surprise Jesus asked her for a drink of water. 'Why are you asking me?' she exclaimed. Soon they were

deep in conversation. The woman's amazement grew as Jesus told her about the work God had given him to do. He even knew all about her, and the wrong things she had done. Greatly impressed, she went home to bring her friends to meet Jesus.

After this Jesus returned to Capernaum. The Roman army had a garrison there, and the Roman officer in charge was a good, just man. He even built a synagogue where Jewish people could worship God.

One day the officer's servant became ill. Sad and worried, the officer decided to ask Jesus for help. He went to meet him as he came into the town. Quickly he told Jesus what was wrong.

'I will come and make your servant well,' said Jesus. The officer replied at once, 'No, sir, I don't deserve to have you in my house, and you don't need to come! I know you are under God's authority, just as I am under my commander. I give orders, too, and the soldiers under me obey at once. Just give the order, and my servant will recover.'

Jesus was amazed. 'I have never met any of my people who believes like this! Go home!' he told the officer. 'What you have believed will indeed happen.'

At that very moment the servant became well.

Besides Matthew and the fishermen, Jesus chose seven other men to be his close friends. One day he called them all together, and gave them their own work to do. He sent them off in twos all through the countryside to tell everyone about God's love and to heal the sick. They were not to carry anything with them – no

money, no food, no extra clothing, no bag, no shoes – not even a stick to lean on. People they helped would give them what they needed, because they were doing God's work. So the men set off. They taught people about God, and made the sick well.

A young man pushed through the crowd to Jesus. He was well-fed and well-dressed. His beard was carefully cut and combed. He used perfumes, unlike the poor and the sick who crowded round Jesus. Yet there was something the rich man needed, too. He knelt before Jesus and explained what it was. He wanted to go to heaven when he died. 'What must I do?' he asked Jesus. 'You must keep God's commandments,' answered Jesus.

'I have obeyed them all my life, Teacher!'
Jesus looked very lovingly at the young man.
'There is still one thing – sell your possessions.
Give the money to the poor, and follow me,'
Jesus said warmly. The young man shook his
head. It was too hard for him. He went away
slowly, feeling very sad.

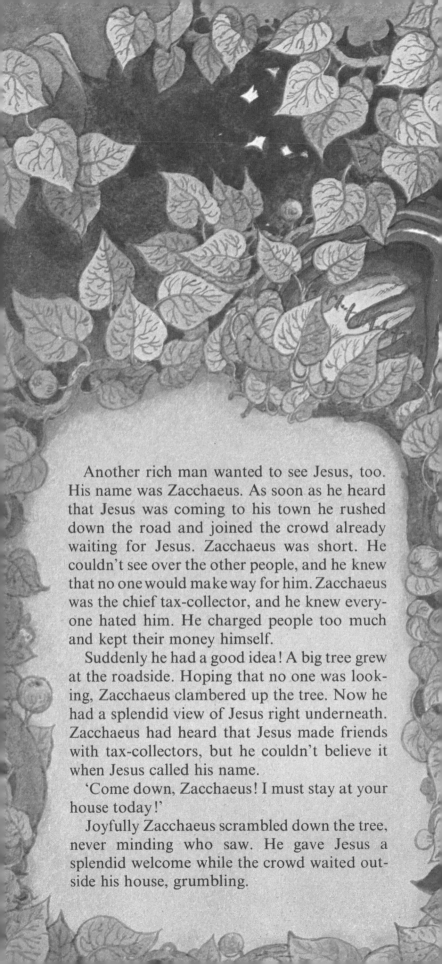

Another rich man wanted to see Jesus, too. His name was Zacchaeus. As soon as he heard that Jesus was coming to his town he rushed down the road and joined the crowd already waiting for Jesus. Zacchaeus was short. He couldn't see over the other people, and he knew that no one would make way for him. Zacchaeus was the chief tax-collector, and he knew everyone hated him. He charged people too much and kept their money himself.

Suddenly he had a good idea! A big tree grew at the roadside. Hoping that no one was looking, Zacchaeus clambered up the tree. Now he had a splendid view of Jesus right underneath. Zacchaeus had heard that Jesus made friends with tax-collectors, but he couldn't believe it when Jesus called his name.

'Come down, Zacchaeus! I must stay at your house today!'

Joyfully Zacchaeus scrambled down the tree, never minding who saw. He gave Jesus a splendid welcome while the crowd waited outside his house, grumbling.

Then the grumbles changed to loud cheers! Zacchaeus had started giving his things away! 'Come on!' he called. 'Help yourselves. Have I cheated anyone here? Take this, then, take four times as much!' When he went back inside, his house seemed bare, but Jesus was there, smiling and pleased. 'Well done,' he said to Zacchaeus.

Jesus knew he had made many enemies who wanted to kill him. Often he warned his friends that he would be put to death, but that God would bring him to life again. One day Jesus took Peter, James and John into the hills. They climbed a high, lonely mountain, and Jesus went ahead to pray. As the fishermen watched they saw his face was shining with light. His clothes dazzled them with a whiteness brighter than snow in sunshine. Jesus stood, splendid with light, and two men stood talking to him. They were Moses and Elijah, two long-dead leaders of the past. Amazed, Simon called out.

At that moment a shining cloud covered them,
and from it came the voice of God himself:
'This is my dear Son. Listen to him!'

The fishermen fell on their faces in fear.
When they looked up, the cloud, Moses and
Elijah had gone. Only Jesus stood beside them,
telling them not to be afraid. Slowly they went
down the mountain. Now they knew that Jesus
really was God's Son, but it was only after he
had been raised from death that they under-
stood the meaning of what they had seen.

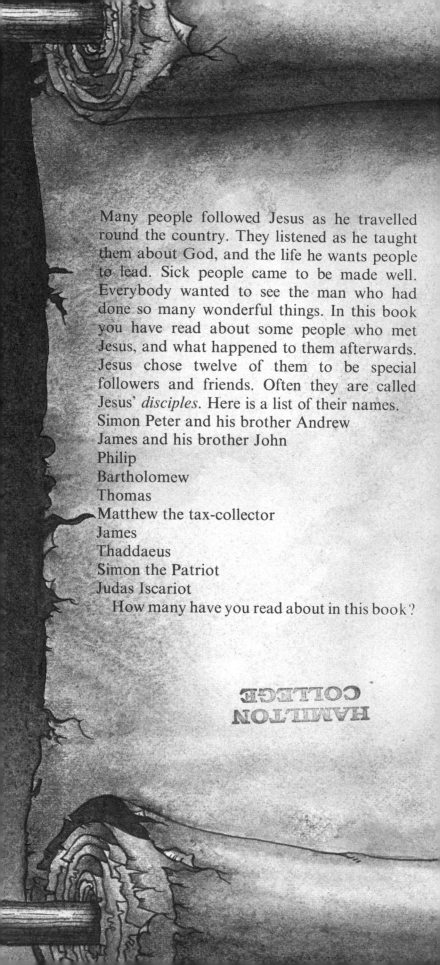

Many people followed Jesus as he travelled round the country. They listened as he taught them about God, and the life he wants people to lead. Sick people came to be made well. Everybody wanted to see the man who had done so many wonderful things. In this book you have read about some people who met Jesus, and what happened to them afterwards. Jesus chose twelve of them to be special followers and friends. Often they are called Jesus' *disciples*. Here is a list of their names.

Simon Peter and his brother Andrew
James and his brother John
Philip
Bartholomew
Thomas
Matthew the tax-collector
James
Thaddaeus
Simon the Patriot
Judas Iscariot

How many have you read about in this book?